DESPERATE DAN

(First Dandy appearance - 1937)

The toughest cowboy in the Wild Wild West, Desperate Dan is a legend in his own lifetime. Dan lives in the remote prospecting town of Cactusville with his Aunt Aggie, the only person who can bake a cow pie to Dan's satisfaction.

COW PIE

KEYHOLE KATE

(First Dandy appearance - 1937)

This little girl with a big nose is always getting in trouble – because she can't mind her own business! If there's a keyhole to be peeped through, or a conversation to be eavesdropped, Kate's in like a flash!

THE BANANA BUNCH

(First Dandy appearance - 2000)

Best of friends (even if they do fight all the time), Brainy, Fatty, Mitzy, Titch, Lanky and Dimmy are The Banana Bunch, a gang of kids intent on having fun, hanging out and surviving the repeated assaults of the unruly Mulligan Mob.

CORPORAL CLOTT

(First Dandy appearance - 1960)

Clott is a well-meaning, enthusiastic soldier who likes nothing better than to use his initiative. Which makes him an absolute nightmare for his superior officer, Colonel Grumbly!

MEET TH

CUDDLES & DIMPLES

Cute, cuddly and well-behaved, they aren't! Two of the most mischievous miscreants ever to grace the pages of a comic!

(First Dandy appearance - 1984)

BULLY BEEF AND CHIPS

(First Dandy appearance - 1967)

Poor Chips! Bully Beef's sole aim in life is to give him a good beating up! Luckily, Chips is a clever chap and usually manages to get his own back!

JOCKS AND THE GEORDIES

(First Dandy appearance - 1975)

By the time you read this, Scotland may have opted for independence. Whatever the outcome of the referendum, I'm sure these lads will keep fighting – just for old times' sake!

BRAIN DUANE

(First Dandy appearance - 1994)

The little boy with the big brain, Duane is always inventing amazing contraptions to make his life better. And they always go wrong…

GREEDY PIGG

(First Dandy appearance – 1965)

Mr Pigg likes nothing better than confiscating the contents of his pupils' lunchboxes! A man of awesome appetite and no scruples, Pigg is the class glutton!

THE SMASHER

(First Dandy appearance – 1958)

Clumsy rather than destructive, unlucky rather than scheming, The Smasher leaves a trail of carnage behind him wherever he goes!

BERYL THE PERIL

(First Dandy appearance – 1993)

Trouble is never far away when Beryl the Peril is around!

BRASSNECK

(First Dandy appearance – 1964)

Charley's uncle created Brassneck to keep him company. A faithful friend, Brassneck is also lumbered with fragile electronics which can be knocked awry by the slightest of impacts!

E STARS!

BING BANG BENNY

(First Dandy appearance – 1956)

Benny loves only one thing more than dynamite – blowing things up with dynamite!

WINKER WATSON

(First Dandy appearance – 1961)

Top wangler at Greytowers School, Winker is the pupils' best defence against their greedy, conniving and downright nasty form master, Mr Creep…

LETTER FROM THE EDITOR

HI, READERS, AND WELCOME TO THE DANDY ANNUAL 2015! IN THE FOLLOWING PAGES YOU'LL FIND HEROES, VILLAINS, SCHEMERS, IDIOTS, SCRAPPERS AND RASCALS. SOME ARE BRAVE, SOME ARE CLUMSY, SOME ARE NOSEY, SOME ARE… WELL, A LITTLE DIM. WHATEVER THEY ARE, THEY'RE SURE TO HAVE YOU HOOTING WITH LAUGHTER AS THEY GO ABOUT THEIR DANDY BUSINESS.
ENJOY THE DANDY ANNUAL, AND WE'LL SEE YOU AGAIN NEXT YEAR!
THE DANDY EDITOR

My uncle BLACK HOLE BERT is a scientist! He's offered to show me around his research facility! Perhaps I'll peek through the keyholes at their top secret stuff!

TOP SECRET SCIENTIFIC PLACE

KEEP OUT

SHH!

AUTHORIZED PERSONNEL AND DANDY CHARACTERS ONLY

There'll be none of your obsessions with keyholes here, Kate! The doors only use keycards!

PROFESSOR BLACK HOLE BERT'S LABORATORY

GLOOM

BEEP!

Aw no! This is gonna be a boring visit!

However, perhaps you'd be interested in seeing the TIME MACHINE I've invented?

WOW! It's keyhole-shaped!

Is it? I hadn't really noticed!

Does it work? Can I have a go?

VWOOP! VWOOP! VWOOP...

I thought that might interest her! I wonder what time periods she'll visit?

Later... or rather, EARLIER, as we're now in the distant past...

VWOOP! VWOOP!

Huh! I wonder what time I've travelled back to? There aren't any keyholes here!

COOL! There's a massive keyhole-shaped...

...d...d... DINOSAUR!

OI! Can't I sit and admire the sunset without some funny monkey annoying me?

I'm in prehistoric times...and it's his DINNER TIME! I'm off!

LEW STRINGER

I wonder what time I'll visit next?

Find out later in this book!

The SMASHER

LEW STRINGER

The BANANA BUNCH

Clott, you buffoon, stop pretending to be a woodland pixie and come down out of that tree. I have a job for you.

I think there's potential for a woodland pixie division in the British Army, Colonel Grumbly, Sir. We can have magic wands and uniforms made out of flower petals.

That's a good idea, Clott. I'll write it down and file it with all your other ideas in a great big bin that's on fire. Now listen carefully...

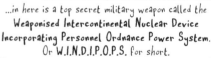

...in here is a top secret military weapon called the **Weaponised Intercontinental Nuclear Device Incorporating Personnel Ordnance Power System.** Or **W.I.N.D.I.P.O.P.S.** for short.

TOP SECRET

CORPORAL CLOTT

WINDIPOPS?

Yes, Clott, WINDIPOPS.

Later...

I've never seen anyone laugh so hard they've turned themselves inside-out before, Clott.

It hurt quite a bit, Sir.

Stop whining, Clott. Now, I want you to guard the WINDIPOPS.

We have information that the enemy want to steal it.

Ho-ho-ow!

The top brass told me it would be foolish to let the most stupid, ignorant, dense, simpleminded, idiotic, thick, dimwitted, dumb, dopey, moronic, pea-brained, half-witted, boneheaded soldier in the entire army guard a top secret weapon worth trillions of pounds, but I decided not to listen to them for some reason.

Thank you, Sir.

Hold your horses, Clott! You must first prove to me that I have made the right choice.

I want you to guard this egg! You must keep it safe for a whole week and then I'll let you guard the WINDIPOPS.

Yes, Sir! You can trust me. I'll guard that egg with my life!

Whoa, there, Clott! I think you're getting ahead of yourself wth all this fancy talk of guarding things with your life.

Before you guard the egg, you must first prove to me that you are worthy, by guarding this brick for a whole day!

Alexander Matthews

THEM'S FIGHTING WORDS!

```
K  I  C  K  Y  H  C  N  U  P
A  G  U  L  S  T  S  O  C  K
P  O  L  L  A  H  W  U  N  N
O  U  C  H  A  W  H  U  P  A
W  S  M  K  I  A  L  W  O  P
K  Z  E  M  M  C  F  W  T  S
M  I  A  M  E  K  F  F  O  A
T  A  E  B  A  L  U  T  I  H
C  R  A  C  K  R  C  P  O  B
```

THE BOYS ARE IN
DETENTION UNTIL
THEY CAN FIND THE
WORDS BELOW.
CAN YOU HELP THEM?

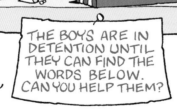

HOWL WHALLOP KAPOW PUMMEL HAMMER SHAKE
POW SOCK HIT THWACK SPANK KICK SLUG
AIM CLUNK PUNCH CLAW CRACK OUCH BEAT
BOP BIFF WHUP MAIM RAM PUSH CUFF

DETENTION
SLIPS

Oooff!!

THONK!

Blither!!!

WUMP!

That's a great idea, Dad. I'll slap the wallpaper paste on thickly...

SPLOTCH!

...then stick Firmly to the wall!

Oops, I think I may have gotten a little carried away.

You think?!

GGGRRRR! COME HERE, YOU LITTLE PEST!!

First he wants me to go - now he wants me to stay! See you later, Dad. Much later!

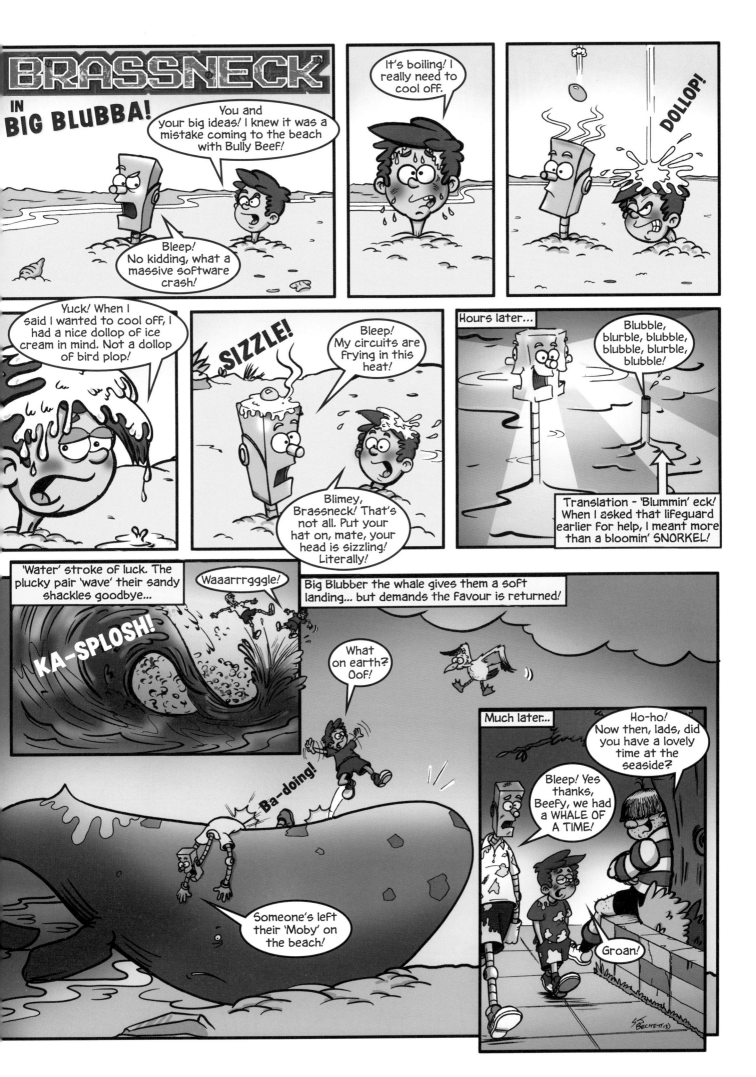

CORPORAL CLOTT

Windipops are vital for the safety of this country, Grumbly!

Yes, General, although they do smell a bit.

Not that sort of windipops, Grumbly! I was referring to the robotic armour that was entrusted to you and has recently been stolen.

Oh! I thought you meant the sort that come out of your bum and make a funny sound. Not to worry, General, I'll put my best man on the case! It won't be long before I find where the enemy are hiding their windipops!

Well I suppose they hide them up their bottoms, Colonel.

I meant the armour, General.

Ah, of course! It's all very confusing. I sometimes think we could have come up with a better name for it.

Soon...

Captain, you are one of the bravest, most capable soldiers in the entire army and I need your help.

Give this to Corporal Clott, please.

ORDERS

I've asked Clott to find some of the roughest, toughest mercenary soldiers in the fighting business for this mission. I wonder who he'll recruit? Perhaps...

...Jenkins The Butcher. Lost an eye in a fight with 12 killer bears with big swords taped to their arms. The bears came off worse.

Colin 'Killer' McKillerson. This man is so dangerous that the enemy surrendered when they heard his name read out on the radio after he texted in a funny story about his cat.

Frank 'Hammerface' Bloodbath. He had his whole head replaced with a huge hammer which he uses to smash his enemies — and to put up shelves for keeping his collection of china piglets on.

Yoo-hoo, Colonel! I've assembled the team. They're outside.

That was quick. I'll come and inspect them immediately.

A better group of men you'd be hard pushed to find, Colonel Grumbly, Sir.

Alexander Matthews

Explain to me, Clott, how it is that when I asked you to recruit tough mercenaries you instead recruited this lot.

I can't explain, Colonel, and that's why we are called **The Unexplainables!**

The word is 'inexplicable', not 'unexplainable', Clott.

Oh right. We are called **The Inexplicables!**

This is Chris. He's our heavy weapon expert. He's familiar with all sorts of weapons including breadcrumbs and, umm, ponds.

This is Billy Parsons, my nephew. I haven't told him that he's in the army now because he might tell his mum and that will get me into trouble.

And this is our stealth expert, Mr Strawface. It will be his job to creep silently about and to scare away any crows that might try to mess things up.

Well, it's too late to find new soldiers now, I suppose. Get them trained up, Clott. Britain is counting on you! This mission simply must be a success.

Yes, Sir! Wait, what mission? I thought you wanted me to assemble a team of people to organise your birthday party.

I must admit I didn't read this properly.

ORDERS

CLOTT!!!

This is how you avoid an angry enemy soldier, men.

BRASSNECK

Wow! Brassneck, I can't believe I was picked to look after Amadeus during the hols! I'm sooooo excited!

Bleep! Rather you than me, pal! Everyone knows Amadeus is Mr Snodgrass's pride and joy! I hope you get him back in one piece, for your sake!

School's out for the summer and Charley Brand has been charged with the task of looking after Amadeus, the school rat, during the holidays.

It's only a rat, what could possibly go wrong?

Eh?

KER-CHANG!

Bully Beef! I might have known!

Bleep! Er... Charley, I calculate you have a problem.

AMADEUS! NOOOOOO! I haven't even left the school grounds yet!

Don't worry, pal. My heat-sensitive vision will help me scope out the critter.

Bleep! Target located, he's heading into the gym!

GYMNASIUM

Good grief! This is no time for a work out, Amadeus!

Bloop! Epic Fail!

Blummin' eck! Amadeus is more agile than a Russian gymnast!

CRASH!

MOVE IT, OLD MAN WITH A SHOVEL, I CAN'T...

SWOO

SH

...STTTOOOOOOPPPPP!!!

GLOP

Oh, you just know what's going to happen now, don't you?

FWIP

BRRR! How can I enjoy a day free of that peril when I've got a ch-ch-chill?

CRASH TINKLE SMASH KRUNCH WHALOP!

It's not enough you've chilled me to the b-b-bone, you've done it to the whole house t-t-too!

Hey! Don't blame me! If you'd listened to me, the headmaster and the teachers you'd have me stay at home all the time!

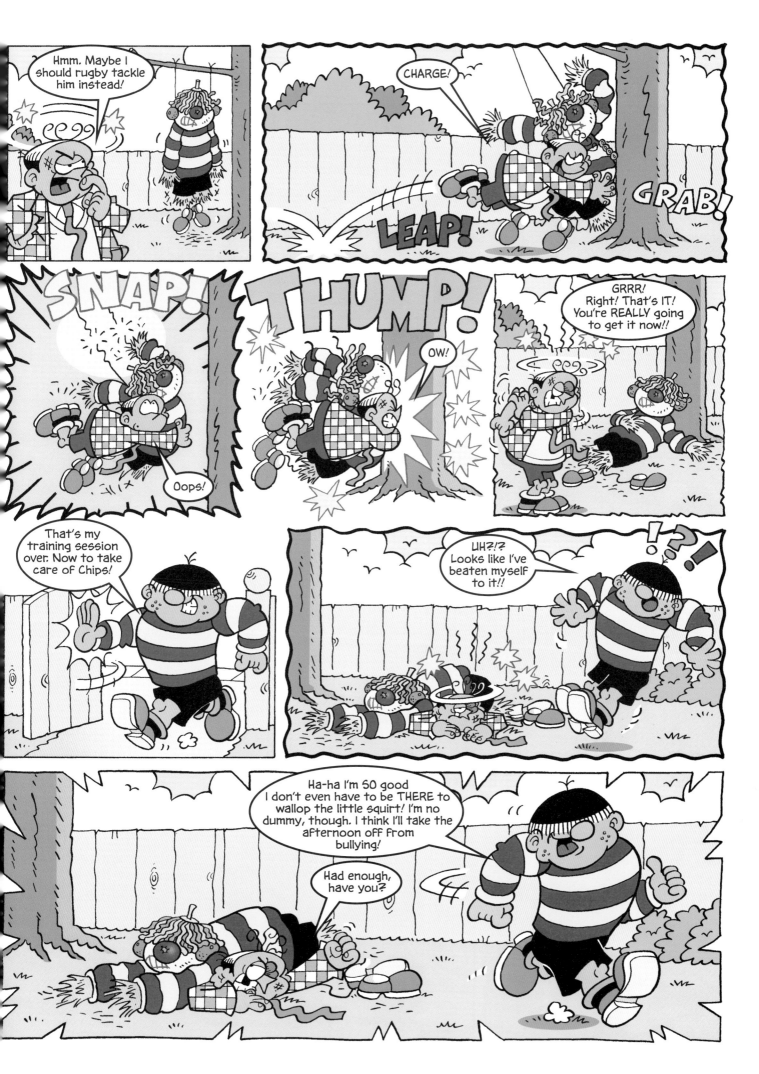

The TIME MACHINE is bringing me to another place!

I wonder what year it is? I'll check out the date on a comic in that shop!

I. FOLDEM NEWSAGENT

COMICS

DANDY N°1 ON SALE TODAY!

It's 1937! Wow! There should be LOTS of keyholes to nosey at around here!

DANDY

Hey! You remind me of me! Let's go keyhole snooping!

Cool! This must be my great-great grandma when she was a young girl! The ORIGINAL Keyhole Kate!

The door to the baker's is my favourite! The smell of fresh bread drifts through the keyhole!

Nice one, but I'd prefer pizza!

BAKE HOUSE

The side door to the cinema is a good one! You can get a free peek at the latest films through this keyhole!

LAUREL & HARDY

THE MARX BROTHERS

RITZ

In black and white, and no downloads?

Pizza? Downloads? What is this strange girl talking about?

Let's peek through this shed door keyhole to see what's inside!

NOOOO! Don't look through that one!

Come on! You should know Keyhole Kate never resists a keyhole!

I always resist THAT keyhole!

AAAGH!

I'll never un-see that!

It's not a shed! It's an outside toilet!

FLUSHHH!

WC

STINK!

WHIFF!

GRR! How dare you?

URRRGH! I think I've seen enough of the 1930's! TIME to move on!

LEW STRINGER

See Kate's final journey in time later in this book!

Eventually, the big night arrives.

All set, lads?

You would never be so foolish as to sail to France alone?

YOU WOULD NEVER BE SO FOOLISH AS TO SAIL TO FRANCE ALONE?

LET HARM COME TO THAT BOY? LADY BLAKENEY, I WILL SAVE ARMAND!

Do you think I would ever let harm come to that boy? Lady Blakeney, I will save Armand.

The interval. Backstage.

You know what, chaps? You look tired. This is a bit of a toil for some of you, isn't it?

No, Winker! We don't mind!

We're only too happy to do it, Winker, after all you've done for us over the years!

No, I've been selfish! This is too much like jolly hard work for too many of you! I've got a different idea for the final act. We'll just make it up as we go along!

Er, are you sure, Winker? That sounds terrifying!

Don't worry, lads! You just follow my lead, we'll just have a jolly big sword-fight and enjoy ourselves!

And so...

En garde, Chauvelin! Come any closer and I'll slice off your nose!

En garde!

No, you en garde!

No, you en garde!

And finally...

CLAP CLAP CLAP!

CLAP CLAP CLAP! Bravo! Bravo! CLAP! CLAP! CLAP!

Watson! Boys! What on earth happened? It was as if you made up the last act as you went along!

Sorry, Mr Creep, Sir... though the audience seem happy enough..

Mr Creep? Is that right? Are you the director?

Er, well...

Marvellous production! What you did with the final act was terrifically original, I loved it!

Y-you did?

Absolutely! Subverting the genre in that way, such subtlety, such poetry! Well done, Sir!

Well, I do have a bit of a theatrical background.

It's obvious! I shall give you full praise when I write my review. I did mention I'm a theatre critic, didn't I?

Er, no, I don't believe you did... it's Clarence Creep.

I say, the masters are having a little buffet party to celebrate the play, would you care to join us, Mr — er...?

Pannit. Willy Pannit, theatre critic, at your service. And yes, I'd love to, old boy.

Well, that all went off rather well, Winker!

We're not finished yet, Trotty! Listen carefully...

Fancy the masters having a feed to celebrate the play and not inviting us — the performers!

I know! Their greed simply staggers me.

But at that very moment, in the next room:

En garde! Yes, it's the Scarlet Pimpernel! Hand over all the grub or I'll have someone's eye out!

LEAP

Of all the bally cheek!

We'd better do what he says.

Sob! I shall waste away!

This time Watson has shown his hand! We *know* it's *him* in that costume!

Where is he?!! Oh!

Looking for someone, Mr Creep, Sir?

Watson, I know it was you — where's your costume? And the grub?!

Grub, Mr Creep, Sir? I've no idea what you mean.

But as for my costume, it was there a minute ago, but when I came out of the shower someone had pilfered it.

My guess would be one of the fifth formers

GAH! AND DOUBLE GAH!

A little later:

You make a fine Pimpernel, Trotty!

Not a patch on you, Winker, but those fencing lessons you gave me came in handy!

Bit of luck that chap from the paper coming along and liking the play so much! Otherwise we'd have really been for it!

Gentlemen, I'd like you to meet Squinky's Uncle Boris — he's a professional actor! I thought we might need him... And didn't he play his part magnificently?!

What a lark! Haven't enjoyed myself so much since playing the Fool in King Lear!

See, lads, it's as I said — acting's just a matter of playing the fool for a living!

Your teacher's certainly acting up downstairs!

We'd better get on with hiding the evidence.

Winker is truly a star amongst stars!

Here's to Winker!

Hurrah!

Twelve days till lift off...

Eight days till lift off...

Six days till lift off...

Four days till lift off...

Three minutes till lift off...

Meanwhile...

Brassneck stormed off so quickly, I couldn't keep up! If I can get a fix on him with Brassneck's locator app, I'll go and find him.

Oh, nuts!

SOFTWARE FAILED PRODUCT RECALL IN OPERATION

At the castle...

Ah! Brassneck, at last we meet again.

Bleep! The Maker?

That's right, rust bucket! Although these days I prefer a more menacing moniker. You can call me The Mecha-lo-Maniac! Ha-ha! It's far more befitting for an evil genius such as myself!

GINGER NUTS

Brassneck, my boy, your tired old circuits are way past their use-by-date. I'm afraid it's time you were decommissioned.

Decommissioned?

GINGER NUTS

That's right! Or in simpler terms... DISMANTLED!

Meet Alloy-ears. My brand new state of the art model. He's kitted out with everything a modern robot boy needs. I think your little chum, Charley, would be thrilled to meet him!

Bleep! Ch... Ch... Charley!

Don't fry your circuits worrying just yet... I have one last job for you to do for me, sunshine. Chortle.

Meanwhile....

STUPID PHONE!!! GRRR!

I don't know why you're stressing, Charley, the answer to our problem is

We just need to follow the trail of destruction.

And that will lead us to...

...here? Gulp!

HUMANS BEWARE!

Meanwhile...

The problem with having a massive castle, Brassneck, is the high ceilings are a nightmare to keep clean! Oh! You've missed a bit.

Blummin' cheek!

You see Alloy-ears here doesn't quite have the reach!

Decommissioning protocol authorised, Master!

Ah! Excellent!

Hold it right there!

You leave my pal alone!

Eh?

Alloy-ears! Attack this bag of bolts! I will not be threatened in my own massive castle!

SPLAT!

SPLOOSH!

Glub!

Bleeurgh!

BZZZT!

Noooo!

Bleep! Ha-ha! What a drip! Your rubbish new model's not even water-resistant!

Bah! A mere oversight on my part. But now, my old friend, it's time to pull you apart.

SPLURT!

WAAAAAH!

Yeeeeargh! Nooooooo!

Nice work, Brassneck! You're one slick robot!

Hooray!

Come on, let's get out of here!

HEADS

BODIES

THIS
WAY
UP

ARMS

LEGS

The SMASHER

Smasher's aunt and uncle are visiting from Australia...

It's nice to meet Smasher at last! He hadn't been born when we emigrated to Australia!

Tough looking little fella, isn't he?

He was a very cute baby! I'll show you his baby photos!

NOOOO! Not the baby photos!

Here we go! A whole album full of photos of Smasher as a baby!

This is so embarrassing! There goes my street cred!

Dad holding baby Smasher for the first time. Er, Smasher dented his nose with that rattle!

Smasher with his first toy. He'd only had it for five minutes before he broke it!

ODD SHAPED LEARNING TOY

Smasher playing in his pedal tractor. I still get a twinge in that foot!

Smasher's first day at school. He was excluded for a week after that.

SCHOOL

OK. Perhaps he wasn't that cute!

WAHEYY! It wasn't embarrassing after all!

It was for us!

KICK

SMASH!

LEW STRINGER

Maybe it was tempting fate to call him Smasher?

CORPORAL CLOTT

Sniff. You make me so proud, men. I doubt there's anyone finer in the entire British army than you three.

I'm tired. Can I lie on the ground?

Quack.

Quiet in the ranks, you two. Take a tip from Mr Strawface – you don't hear a peep out of him.

Screech!

That's enough, soldier! We'll have no screeching while you're being inspected.

Aaagh!

SCREEECH!

Ok! Ok! You can be in the team! We need a bat!

Soon...

Men, you need to be physically fit for this mission so we're going to do some circuits of the assault course. Watch me first so you know how.

First, the twelve foot wall.

SLAM!

Oo can wun awound ib oo wike.

Alexander Matthews

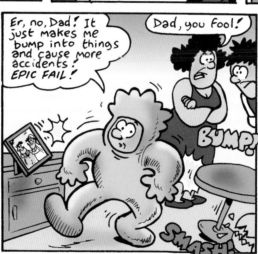

The BANANA BUNCH

SMASHING WORD SEARCH

Smasher's been doing what he does best! Look through the wreckage and work out what Smasher has smashed! Then find the names of the items in the mallet wordsearch!

C	L	O	C	K	L	A	B	O	X	S	T	A	T	U	E
O	F	N	O	T	B	X	O	W	L	I	O	S	O	Y	B
M	G	A	N	P	I	A	N	A	O	B	I	F	O	T	O
P	L	I	A	G	C	C	D	R	O	B	O	T	A	I	H
U	I	P	I	A	Y	O	K	D	Y	H	T	A	V	E	T
T	E	O	E	T	C	M	B	R	S	F	R	C	T	L	E
E	Q	S	H	P	L	P	T	O	A	S	T	E	R	P	L
R	A	C	R	H	E	U	J	B	A	T	H	D	C	I	I
V	V	U	E	V	U	T	J	E	B	B	D	V	S	F	O
P	E	Z	T	E	L	E	V	I	S	I	O	N	F	I	T

Answers: ➡

DIARY OF A GREEDY PIGG

MONDAY

The boys bought me some lovely cakes for being such a wonderful teacher. I insisted the cakes be shared with the entire class.

TUESDAY

I thought I could hear a burning firework fuse from the storeroom. I entered to discover bangers! I put them out and disposed of them safely. I think Jasper was pleased!

WEDNESDAY

Today I was asked to stand in for the games teacher.
I impressed the pupils with my Olympic standard trampolining and groundbreaking dismount!

THURSDAY

The fire alarm mysteriously went off at school! I made sure all the pupils were escorted out of the building and then stayed to check no-one was left behind!

FRIDAY

After another successful week, the headmaster complimented me on a job well done and gave me the afternoon off!

CUDDLES and DIMPLES

You three get this place tidied before I come back from maxing out Dad's credit card at the sales – or else!

Dad, it's Boxing-Boxing-Boxing Day! This will ruin our entire Christmas!

Don't make us do our fair share around the house!

...my in the [?] do the housework while you two have one last gift...

NIGEL PARKINSON

...this virtual reality game, kicking weird alien robot monster butt!

WOW!

EXTREME ALIEN ROBOT MONSTER HOME INVASION IX

COO-OOOL!

Wearing this gear, you'll feel like all the carnage is actually happening!

Wowsers!

Game world...

Oo! Everything does seem real!

Yeah! Breakable too. Cool!

CRUNCH CRUNCH

What's that noise? We're under attack!

Aargh! Take that, killer robot!

ZAP THEM!

ZAP! ZAP!

Real world...

That's it, lads, keep zapping. Scrub out those dreaded alien robots!

CRUNCH CRUNCH

ZAP! ZAP!

With Woodall out the way, the boys beat the Masters by nine runs.

SKREEEEECH!

C'mon, slow coach. That's the third time I've lapped you and you've only done one circuit!

It's no wonder - look at my horse! I've seen My Little Ponies bigger than this!

The book says that you have to kick with your heels into the horses flanks and he'll go faster.

I have been!

Perhaps we should try something else...

WHAT? WAIT! NO!! THAT'S A PEA SHOOTER!!

DAKA-DAKA-DAKA-DAKA!

Wow, that's better! He's gone through the jumps, crashed into the wall, half drowned in the water jump... way to go, Dad and Thumper!

NOOOOO! AHHH! HELP! OOF!

That was sooooo cool! Can we go again?

ONCE, JUST ONCE, I'D LIKE TO GO HOME IN THE SAME TRANSPORT WE ARRIVED IN! WHIMPER!

Wow! I didn't know you could move like that!

Neither did I!

HOME

CORPORAL CLOTT

Alexander Matthews

The BANANA BUNCH